Anu in Bangladesh

Naila Kabeer and Olivia Bennett

Photographs by Prodeepta Das

A & C Black · London

Hello! I'm Anu. I live in Bangladesh. Our flat is on the outskirts of Dhaka, the capital city. It's on the top floor of a two-storey house and we share a garden with the families who live on the ground floor.

Our part of the city is called Narayanganj and it is built along the banks of the river Sitalakhya. There are lots of factories and warehouses in Narayanganj. The river is always busy, with boats carrying cargo to and from Bangladesh and ports all over the world.

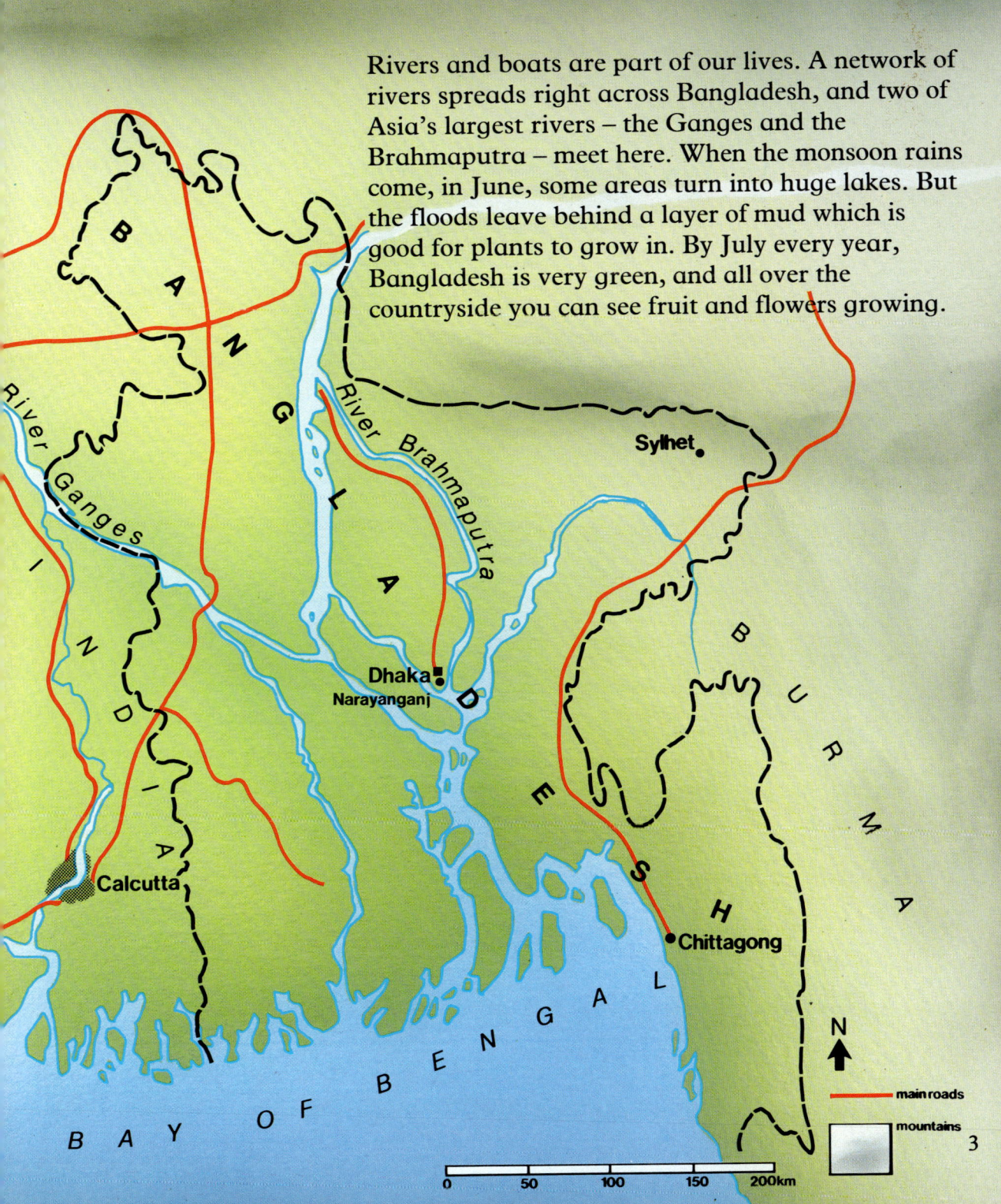

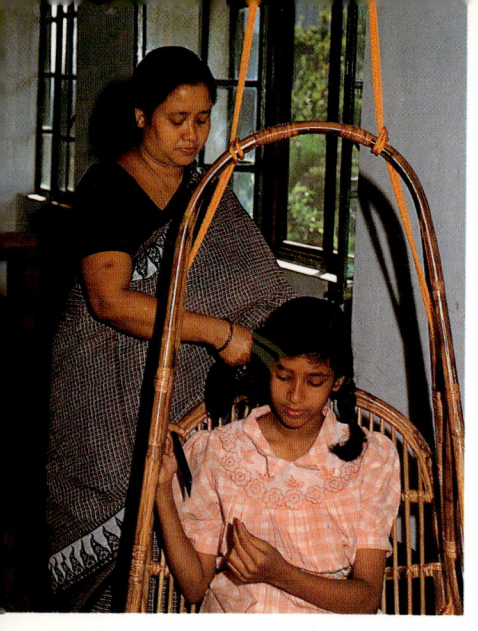

Every morning, Mum and I sit on the verandah while Mum does my hair. The verandah runs the length of the house and all the other rooms lead off it. In summer, there's always a cool breeze blowing in through the verandah windows.

I share a room with my sister, Kona. She's fourteen. I'm twelve, nearly thirteen. Kona and I are good friends and we spend a lot of time together, playing games. Ludo is one of our favourites. Our brother, Rana, is sixteen. He's studying hard now, and we don't see much of him.

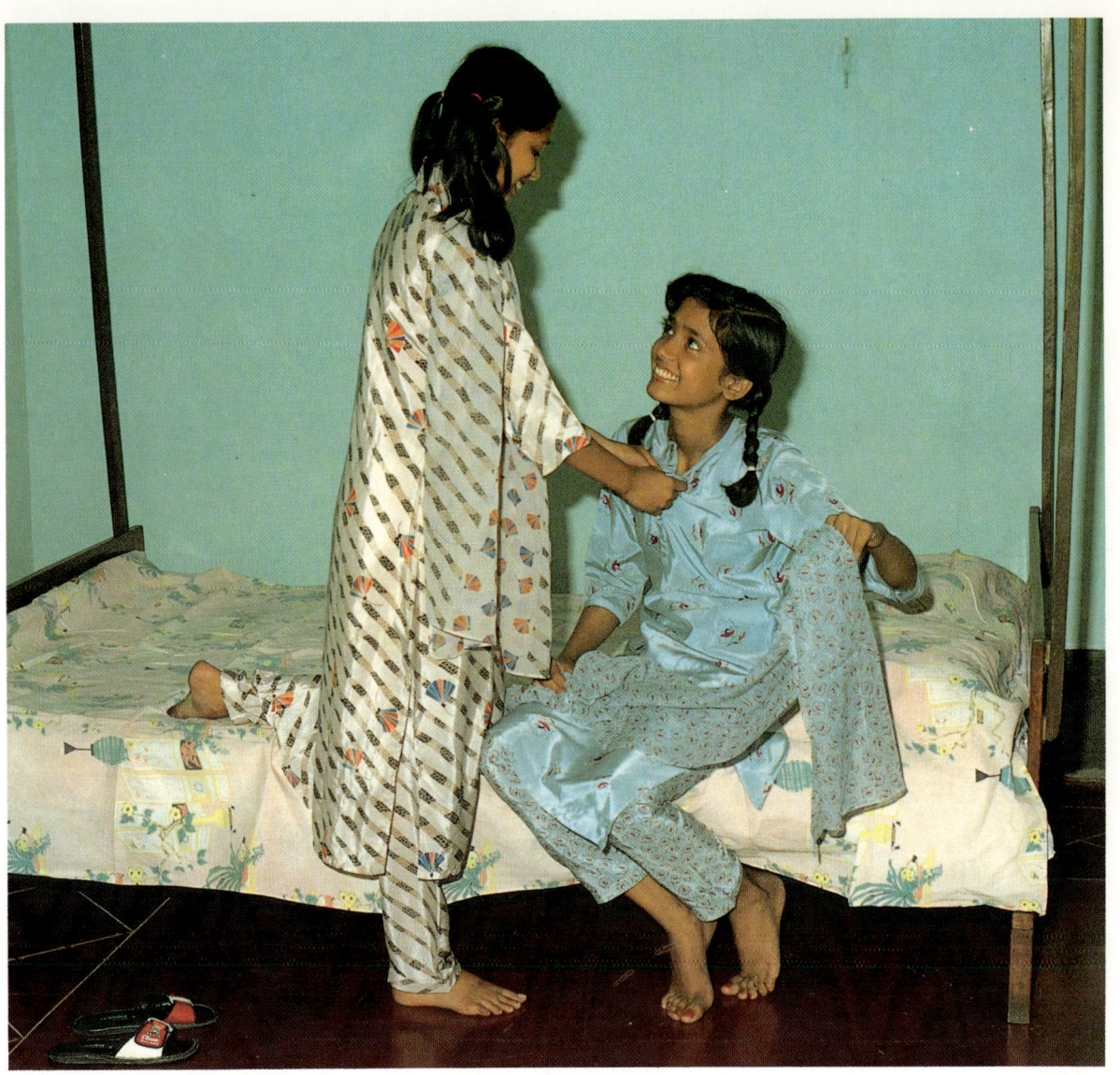

Because it is January, and the coolest time of year, Kona and I need warm jerseys in the evening. But during the day we wear cotton dresses. For prayers and for school we wear shalwar kameez – long tunics and loose trousers. When we're older, about fifteen, we'll wear shalwar kameez all the time, and when we're seventeen or so we'll wear saris.

In December and January we have school holidays. Today Mum and I are going shopping together, so we take a bicycle rickshaw.

There must be millions of rickshaws in Bangladesh, and sometimes they all seem to be heading for the same place as we are! At least, that's what it feels like when we get stuck in a traffic jam, with everybody shouting and fiercely ringing their bells!

Bicycle rickshaws are always wonderfully decorated. They are covered with paintings of mosques, birds, flowers, animals, famous film stars or politicians.

First we go to a kaporer dokan to buy some material. Inside the shop, the shelves are piled high with coloured cloth. There's one pattern I'd like to have a closer look at.

'That lovely purple one, please, with the little red flowers.' The shopkeeper gets it down for me. I wonder whether Mum will let me have it for my new dress.

Mum's in a good mood this morning. She buys the material I like and then I persuade her to buy me some matching bangles as well. To fit the bangles on, you have to make your hand very narrow by squashing your thumb on to your palm.

Next we go to a kashar dokan to buy some brass. We need a new water pot and some cooking pans. Brass looks bright and shiny like gold, but it isn't so expensive. The owner puts the pot on his scales to find out the price. The more it weighs, the more it costs.

Shopping is thirsty work. We stop at a stall to buy two green coconuts. The stall-holder slices off the tops so that we can drink from them. Mmm! There's nothing like cool, clear coconut juice when you're feeling hot and thirsty. But you have to be careful: it's hard to drink without dribbling!

In the afternoon, I wander round to my dad's office. I like going to his office because it's in a lovely old building. But mainly I look forward to walking home with Dad when he has finished work. He works for the River Transport Company. He's in charge of hundreds of boats which bring goods to Narayanganj from all over Bangladesh. From Narayanganj, large ships take the goods by sea to other countries, such as Russia, Britain, Germany, Brazil, Japan and China.

At this time of year Dad has a lot to do. Most of the boats are bringing jute to Narayanganj, and the warehouses are full of it.

Jute is a tall plant, grown all over Bangladesh. It looks golden when it's ripe, and that's why there are so many poems and songs about 'sonar Bangladesh' – 'golden Bangladesh'. There are tough fibres in jute stems, which can be dried and twisted together: the jute arriving here will end up as rope, string, sacks and carpet backing.

When I get to Dad's office I have to wait because Dad's having a meeting. I read the newspaper, and wish he'd hurry up. He can't put off the meeting because tomorrow is Friday, the Muslim holy day, and the office will be closed.

When I've read all the interesting bits in the newspaper, I go outside to watch the boatmen. I often come down to the riverside. There's always something to see.

The workmen beat jute on metal stakes to soften it. It looks silky, although the strands actually feel rough and scratchy.

After the jute has been beaten, machines press it together into tight bales, ready to be shipped overseas. Dad says that the machines were built over a hundred years ago in Liverpool! They are very noisy. Jute dust fills the air. The workmen wear scarves over their mouths so that they don't breathe in the dust.

Sometimes Kona and I arrange to meet our friends down here by the river. It's a good place to play Kana Machi, because there's a lot of open space to run about in. 'Kana Machi' means 'Blind Fly'. The fly is the person who has been blindfolded, and who has to try to catch one of the other players.

Everybody else dodges in and out all around the fly. Sooner or later, somebody is too daring and gets caught. Then that person puts on the blindfold, and the game begins again, with the new fly.

I have to be home by six o'clock. Even during the holidays, my sister and I have a tutor who comes to our home four evenings a week. He coaches us in maths and science. I don't mind the extra lessons because all my friends have them too, but I would rather have Bengali lessons than maths.

Bengali is our language. It's a beautiful, poetic language. Last term at school, I wrote a poem about going to visit my grandmother. Then I painted a picture to go with it.

My picture shows part of the village where Grandma lives. Most people in Bangladesh live in small country villages.

I put the river into my picture because it's so important for our visit to Grandma. The only way to reach her is by boat. We can't go at this time of year because it's the dry season and the river which leads past her village is too shallow for boats. Later on, around July, rain will have made the river deep enough for us to go and see Grandma.

On Friday, Dad gets up very early to go to buy food at the bazaar. Women don't go to this busy, noisy market. First Dad buys some fish. Mum has asked him to get rui and rup chanda. I love rui when Mum cooks it in macher jhol. But she may not do macher jhol today – she knows so many different recipes for fish.

After he has bought the fish, Dad buys a bunch of fresh green coriander.

Then Dad goes to a spice stall to buy some ginger and some chillies. After that he only has to get some vegetables – then he can take all the shopping home.

At midday, Dad and Rana go to the local mosque for Friday prayers. We're Muslims, so we pray five times a day. On work days Dad can't get to a mosque, but that doesn't matter. He can always find a quiet place to pray.

Mum and Kona and I don't go to the mosque. We always pray at home. This morning we got up at five o'clock to say our first prayers. As a sign of respect, Kona and I each wear a dupatta over our heads, and shalwar kameez. We kneel on prayer mats facing Makkah, the holy city of Islam in Saudi Arabia, and ask for Allah's blessing.

We always have religious education on Fridays, sometimes from Dad and sometimes from a teacher of Islam. I'm pleased because Dad's teaching us today. We're learning Arabic so that we'll be able to read and recite verses from the Qur'an, our holy book.

Our Friday meal is always special. Today we are going to have some macher jhol, after all. Mum is preparing the ingredients on the balcony at the back of the house.

She has already sifted out any stones and grit from the rice, and now she's scraping the scales off the fish. I like doing that. We use a curved knife called a boti, which has its own legs to stand on. But Mum doesn't often let me have a go. She says I do it too slowly.

When Mum has prepared the rice and the fish, she crushes and grinds the fresh spices into a paste. She uses a sheel batta – a stone rolling-pin. For today's dishes, she needs ginger, garlic, turmeric, cumin and coriander. The bright yellow one is the turmeric.

Mum's a very good cook. If you came round for a meal with us, you'd be offered lots of delicious food. Even if you were very hungry when you arrived, you probably wouldn't be able to finish everything that Mum put on your plate. You'd have to try to make room for it though, or she'd be disappointed.

This evening, Rana takes time off from working for his exams. He gets out the tabla, and I sit at the harmonium. We sing folk songs. The harmonium has keys like a piano and bellows which I squeeze in and out to make the sound. Sometimes I play a wrong note, but nobody minds because we're all having such a good time.

As our school holidays are nearly over, Dad is going to take a day off work so that we can go on a river outing. We hire a small boat with two boatmen. We sit in the shade under the bamboo roof, and the boatmen row, one at either end.

The river is crowded. There are ferry boats crammed with passengers, and cargo boats carrying all kinds of goods: sacks of rice and wheat, clay pots, bamboo poles, and piles of jute. Some of the boats have sails which have been mended so often that they look like patchwork.

We eat our picnic as we go along. While we're tucking in, we see people fishing, bathing and washing clothes in the river. Further on, we pass by farmers working in the fields which stretch down to the water's edge.

After a couple of hours we have left the city behind. We stop at a village and stretch our legs. The houses and the paths are built up on earth platforms. In the rainy season the rice fields below the paths fill with water. The houses almost become islands, connected to each other only by narrow tracks. The water often rises nearly as high as the paths, and from a distance it looks as though people are walking on water!

On the way home, Mum gives me a bag of chana chur – a mixture of nuts and spicy fried and puffed rice. She's kept it a secret until now because she knows that I always eat it up straight away.

As the sun goes down, the two boatmen begin singing songs about the river. 'The river has no beginning, it has no end,' they sing. I feel rather sleepy, and very full of chana chur. Today has been a lovely way to end the holiday.